Potty Animals

What to Know When You've Gotta Go!

To a few of my favorite critters:
Aiden, Gable, Brody, and Ethan.
—H.V.

To little Ada.
—V.P.

ISBN 978-0-545-33328-3

Text copyright © 2010 by Hope Vestergaard.
Illustrations copyright © 2010 by Valeria Petrone. All rights reserved.
Published by Scholastic Inc., 557 Broadway, New York, NY 10012, by arrangement
with Sterling Publishing Co., Inc. SCHOLASTIC and associated logos are
trademarks and/or registered trademarks of Scholastic Inc.

12 11 10 9 8 7 6 5   17 18 19 20 21/0

Printed in the U.S.A.   40

First Scholastic printing, February 2011

The artwork for this book was rendered digitally.
Designed by Chrissy Kwasnik, who always washes her hands before leaving the bathroom

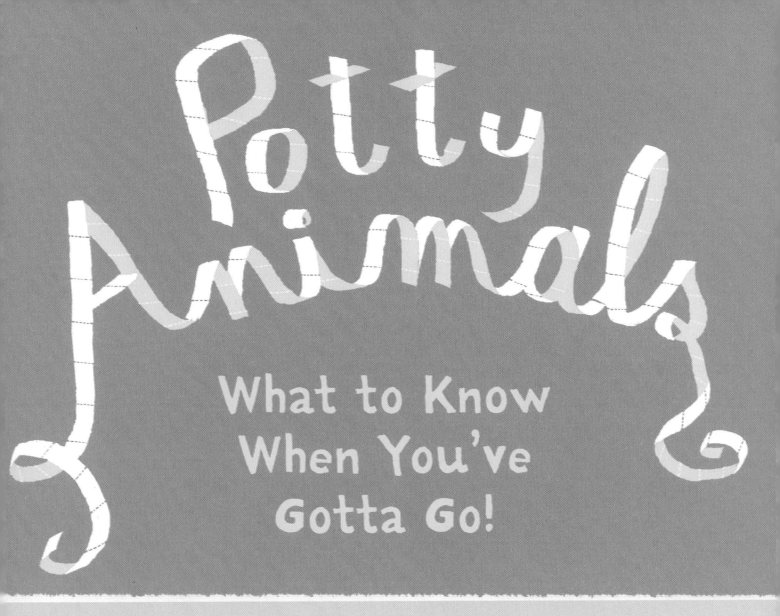

Potty Animals

What to Know When You've Gotta Go!

by Hope Vestergaard

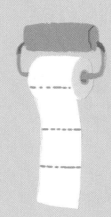

illustrated by Valeria Petrone

SCHOLASTIC INC.
New York   Toronto   London   Auckland
Sydney   Mexico City   New Delhi   Hong Kong

Most critters are quite tidy:
a clean and pleasant lot.
But now and then you'll meet a few
young beasties who are not.

They don't mean to be messy.
They haven't got a clue.
Let's meet some potty animals
and tell them what to do.

Wilbur will not wash his hands—
a habit rather grim.
He doesn't think he picks up germs.
His hands look clean to him!
His parents ask,

his teachers ask,

the other kids ask, too.

And Wilbur always answers,
"I washed my hands, did you?"
His teachers ask if he used soap,
his hands do not smell right.
Eventually, he lathers up—
it's never worth the fight.

Wilbur, always wash with soap!

Wilma tends to wait too long.
She always keeps on playing.
She doesn't want to lose her turn,
or miss what kids are saying.

So Wilma hops from foot to foot.

and waits

and waits.

She waits

And when it's time, she has to race . . . but sometimes she's too late!

Wilma, don't wait!

Though **Arnold** has outstanding aim
to point and kick and throw,
he isn't always accurate
when it is time to go.

He hits the floor, he hits the lid, he hits the toilet seat.
Not much goes in the toilet bowl,
which isn't very neat.

Yuck!
Lift the seat, Arnold!

Freddie is afraid to flush.
He doesn't like the sound.
He worries that he'll get sucked in, and tossed and sloshed around.

So Freddie acts like he forgets.
He hopes that folks won't know
that he's the one who made the mess,
when it's their turn to go.

Don't forget to flush, Freddie!

Helga likes to lollygag,
she's never in a hurry.
But other kids who have to go
can really start to worry.

Sometimes she's having daydreams,
sometimes she's reading books.

Sometimes she's at the mirror
perfecting funny looks.

Hurry up, Helga!

Benji was a barger,
to everyone's chagrin.
He never knocked,
he didn't tap,
he marched straight in.
He had to pee
and didn't see
the critters waiting there.

One day Freddie barged in, too,
and Benji got a scare.

Knock first, Benji!

When it's time to take a trip,
the teacher says to try,
but Roxanne never feels the urge
till cars go whizzing by.

SYCAMORE

Just when the bus gets up to speed,
she says she cannot wait.
It takes so long to stop and go,
she makes the whole class late.

Plan ahead, Roxanne!

Stanley had a secret trick
so he could stay outside.
When he was out and had to go,
Stanley liked to hide.
He'd find a tree and just go pee!

EWW!
It wasn't an emergency,
and no one even knew

until the day that Wilma saw him

tinkle on his shoe.

Stanley, use the toilet!

Sukey gets so thirsty,
she drinks and drinks and drinks.
Then something awful happens
when she catches forty winks.
She dreams of ponds and lakes and rain and floating down a stream,
and when she wakes from naptime...
she finds it's not a dream.

Go potty before you sleep, Sukey!

Georgie often skipped a step:
He didn't like to wipe.
He got an itchy feeling
that made him groan and gripe.

He wished that itch would go away,
but sadly, it did not.
The longer that he waited,
the worse the problem got.

Wipe every time, Georgie!

Farley leaves the door ajar.

He wants to get some air.

But everyone who passes by
just has to
stop
and
stare.

Close the door, Farley!

Agnes has a problem
with bubbles in her belly.
When they come out (and out they come!),
the room can get quite smelly.

Agnes just can't help it,
she has to let them out.
But after several episodes,
it makes her classmates shout:

Excuse yourself, Agnes!

Ziggy can be forgetful
when he is in a rush.
He doesn't forget to lift the seat,
and doesn't forget to flush.

He doesn't forget to wash his hands,
and always turns out the light.
But when he comes out of the bathroom
something's not quite right.

Check your zipper, Ziggy!

Feel free to use our restroom,
and please enjoy your stay!
We like to keep it spic-and-span—
we hope it stays this way.

If you forget your manners,
or don't know what to do,
think about the animals,
and what they'd say to YOU:

Plan ahead!
Don't wait too long!
Go potty before you sleep!
Excuse yourself! Knock first!
Be sure to lift up the seat!

Close the door!
Don't lollygag!
Never forget to wipe!
Wash your hands!
Flush and zip!
Always turn out the light!